THE CRIME LORD

JAK SHADOW

Dorset County Library	
204459125 W	
Askews	2006
	£4.99

Published in the UK in 2006
by Wizard Books, an imprint of Icon Books Ltd.,
The Old Dairy, Brook Road, Thriplow,
Cambridge SG8 7RG
email: wizard@iconbooks.co.uk
www.iconbooks.co.uk/wizard

Sold in the UK, Europe, South Africa
and Asia by Faber and Faber Ltd.,
3 Queen Square, London WC1N 3AU
or their agents

Distributed in the UK, Europe, South Africa
and Asia by TBS Ltd., Frating Distribution Centre,
Colchester Road, Frating Green, Colchester CO7 7DW

Published in Australia in 2006
by Allen & Unwin Pty. Ltd.,
PO Box 8500, 83 Alexander Street,
Crows Nest, NSW 2065

Distributed in Canada by
Penguin Books Canada,
90 Eglinton Avenue East, Suite 700,
Toronto, Ontario M4P 2Y3

ISBN-10: 1-84046-693-6
ISBN-13: 978-1840466-93-5

Typesetting by Hands Fotoset

Printed and bound in the UK by
Clays of Bungay

Contents

Introduction

Last summer you went to a holiday adventure camp. It was fantastic! Instead of teachers, real soldiers, explorers and athletes taught you how to do all kinds of things. You learned how to survive in dangerous lands, how to abseil down a mountain and how to crack secret codes. They even taught you how to track someone cross-country and how to avoid being followed.

On your last day at the adventure camp you were awarded five certificates and told that you were one of the best students they had ever had. You remember that final evening as if it were yesterday and now, with your dangerous mission about to begin, you replay every detail of the scene in your head.

★ ★ ★

After a last campfire and a meal in the open air, one of the sergeants whispers in your ear.

'Colonel Strong would like to see you in his

office. Please follow me. There is nothing to worry about; you haven't done anything wrong.'

You saw Colonel Strong on your first day. He is the officer in charge of the camp, a big man with a booming voice who is more than a little terrifying.

You cannot stop your knees from trembling, and your hands feel cold and clammy as you walk towards his office. You are wondering what on Earth he wants to talk about.

'My people have been watching you all week,' Colonel Strong begins. 'I know you have had a great time here and you've done extremely well. We are all very proud of what you have been able to achieve.'

'It seems that you are exactly what we are looking for. Sit yourself down and let me explain,' he says, pointing to the chair.

'The world is in great danger. More danger than you could possibly imagine,' the colonel continues.

Why is the colonel talking to you like this? He obviously has more to say, so you wait for him to continue.

'My organisation is fighting a secret war against an evil alien genius.'

'But who is he and what does he want?' you ask.

'His name is Triton and he wants to rule the world,' the colonel tells you.

Colonel Strong passes you a photograph of Triton. He is like nothing you have ever seen before. He has

green skin, piercing red eyes, pointed ears, a large nose and has strange lumps on his face. You would have no trouble in picking him out in a crowd.

'I have checked out your history and I have watched you all week. I know that you are loyal, honest and brave, but even so I cannot tell you any more unless you swear a solemn oath to keep this secret.'

You are not too sure what the colonel means, but you know he is trustworthy and you long to hear more. You swear the solemn and binding oath that you will keep the secret.

'I work for an organisation called F.E.A.R.,' the colonel continues. 'It is an organisation so secret that only a handful of people in the whole world know about it.'

'But what is F.E.A.R.?' you ask.

'F.E.A.R. stands for Fighting Evil, Always Ready,' the colonel explains. 'I don't want you to feel you've been tricked, but this activity camp was specially set up to recruit the ideal agent,' he continues. 'We selected only children who we knew would be brave, strong, honest and, above all, quick-witted. We have watched you this week, and out of all the children, you are the one we have picked. We want you to become a F.E.A.R. agent.'

'Agent! What sort of agent? A secret agent?' you shout.

'Yes, a very secret agent. But I can only tell you more if you agree to join us. Or would you prefer it if we just forgot this conversation?'

'Of course I want to help, but I'm only a child. What could I possibly do?' you ask.

'All of our agents are children now. Triton has captured all our best adult agents, but he does not yet suspect our children.'

'Why can't we just hunt him down and kill him?' you reply.

'I wish it were that easy. The world Triton comes from is millions of miles from our planet, but somehow he has managed to get to Earth. He has a time machine and he is trying to change our time and our future. We have to stop him. We managed to capture one of his time machines and we've copied it, so now we've got one of our own.'

'You can count on me,' you say, smiling at the colonel.

'If you agree to become a F.E.A.R. agent you will begin your training during the school holidays. You have been sworn to secrecy, and must not tell anyone about the work you are doing. We will tell your parents as much as they need to know, but no more.'

★ ★ ★

Over the holidays since, your training has been completed. You have worked hard and learned much. You know more about Triton now, especially the fact that he uses a time chip to take him back to a particular time and place. If you can take it from him, or destroy it, he will have to leave. F.E.A.R. have made a chip locator and on every mission you will take one with you. It will help you to find Triton.

Now you are ready to begin your mission, but Colonel Strong's words are ringing in your ears: 'Remember you are facing a most dangerous challenge and an evil enemy.'

You wait for your instructions.

How to Play

Before you start, the colonel will tell you as much as F.E.A.R. know about Triton's plans.

This is not like a normal book. Each section of the book is numbered. At the end of each section you will have a choice to make. Each of these choices will send you to a different section of the book. You make the choices and decide how you are going to deal with Triton.

If you fail, your mission will end and Triton will be able to continue his plan to take over the world. If you manage to combat all of the dangers Triton presents, you will defeat him and the world will be safe – until he strikes in another time and another place! The world needs you.

Your Mission

You arrive at the F.E.A.R. base, expecting to see Colonel Strong waiting for you. But instead Sergeant Harris, the colonel's most trusted soldier, meets you in his jeep and drives you off to Colonel Strong's office.

'The colonel is sorry he's not here. He has been in his office for the past eight hours, staring at the computer screen and looking at maps of London,' the sergeant explains.

'What's happening?' you ask.

'Triton's turned up in London in 1881 and we can't figure out why or what he's up to,' answers the sergeant.

When you reach the colonel's office it is a shambles. There are maps, papers and books scattered everywhere. It looks as if the colonel has not washed or shaved for a couple of days and he seems to be very tired.

'I'm sorry about not meeting you and the

state of my office,' he begins. 'I just can't work this one out.'

'What's the situation?' you ask.

'Triton's set himself as some kind of crime lord in 1881. He is in London, leading a gang of child thieves. They just seem to be breaking into houses and stealing. But we're not sure why or what's behind it all,' the colonel tells you, handing you a photograph of Triton. Triton has a top hat, fake sideburns and he is wearing a pair of tiny glasses on the end of his fat nose.

'So you think he's up to something else?' you ask.

'Well, yes. I've checked everything, like important people of the time, but I've just drawn a blank. We've spent the last 24 hours going through hundreds of books, websites on the Internet and our databases. Nothing important was invented then and there were no major wars either. I just can't figure it out,' the colonel replies, holding his head in his hands.

'What do you want me to do?' you say, hoping that you can help in some way.

'Well, I've already sent Agent 92. Her name is Frankie. I've told her to collect information, but not to tackle Triton and leave that to you,' he answers.

'So I need to find Frankie and see what she knows and then track down Triton and discover what he's up to?' you say, almost to yourself.

'Yes and then deal with him,' the colonel tells you.

'What if I can't find Frankie?' you ask.

'That shouldn't stop you,' answers the colonel. 'It seems that most of the child thieves in London are either working for Triton or know someone who is working for him.'

'I suppose the best thing is to try to join Triton's gang and find out what his plans are,' you suggest.

'Excellent idea! Frankie should be able to help, but she's not trained like you. She won't be able to deal with Triton himself. That's down to you,' the colonel explains.

'When do I go?' you ask.

'First thing in the morning. You've got to try to meet Frankie early at Covent Garden market,' says the colonel. 'In our day it is full of trendy shops and tourists, but in 1881 it was a proper market selling flowers and fruit and veg. Right now, we'd both better try to get some sleep. Sergeant Harris will show you to your room and I'll see you over a very early breakfast.'

★ ★ ★

Sergeant Harris wakes you up at three o'clock in the morning. But even then you have only just enough time to eat some cereal and toast with the colonel before he tells you that a helicopter is waiting.

You are whisked into central London, landing directly in front of a church in the heart of Covent Garden. The helicopter has barely touched the ground when you and the colonel scramble out and head for a huge truck.

The time machine has been fitted inside the enormous body of the truck, with enough space for the scientists and technicians. All around the time chamber there are computers, screens and switches, with several F.E.A.R. agents and scientists busy at work.

'This is going to be tricky, because we can't transport you through time to somewhere where you won't be seen. The best we can hope for is that you appear behind a market stall,' the colonel explains to you. 'And don't worry, if you get into any real danger we can whip you back here in a split second. Swallow this tracker and we will always know where you are and what is happening to you.'

You swallow the tiny capsule and you are certain that the colonel will keep his word.

Now read paragraph **1** to begin your adventure.

1

'Let's get you dressed in 1880s clothes first.
Just go behind the screen where your clothes
are all ready and waiting for you,' says the
colonel.

You can smell something unpleasant before
you even get behind the screen. To your horror,
the clothes laid out for you are barely more
than rags, and they are filthy too.

'Colonel, you could have washed these! Who
wore them last, a pig?' you shout from behind
the screen.

'I'm sorry about that, but you can't go
to the 1880s smelling sweet and clean.
Remember you've got to pass yourself off
as a street child and thief,' the colonel shouts
back.

You pull on the rags and gradually get used
to the awful smell. The colonel can't help
smiling when you come from behind the screen
and you can see that he can smell you because
his nose is twitching.

'First I'll give you the chip locator. We've
sewn a special pocket
inside your trousers,
so it shouldn't fall
out. You may take
one other item with you. Here are three things
that you could take, but you can only choose
one of them,' says the colonel.

On the table is a pocket watch. If you would
like to choose this, turn to **98**. Next to the watch
is a whistle, which could be useful. If you want
to choose the whistle, turn to **75**. The last
choice is a walking stick. If you would like to
pick this, turn to **52**.

2

You grab the policeman's wrist and twist it
round, making him break his hold on you. He
yells out and his other hand grabs for his
truncheon. As he is about to bring it down on
your head you suddenly see strange shapes

pass before your eyes and you feel yourself falling, falling, falling.

You find yourself on the floor of the time chamber and see Colonel Strong's face peering through the glass. Your mission is over. Strong promised that you would not come to any harm and he has kept his promise. The colonel opens the door and helps you to your feet.

'It seems I've failed. Perhaps it wasn't a good idea to tackle the policeman. But we could try it all again, couldn't we?' you suggest to the colonel.

If you would like to try the mission once again, go back to **1**.

3

Two of Triton's henchmen are guarding the front door and there are another two at the back door, so you slip into the downstairs toilet, pull up the window and sneak out. You jump down into the garden and walk around the side of the house. It is very foggy and you hope you haven't been seen, but you have a strange feeling that you are being followed.

'Stop! Where are you going?' commands a voice in the fog.

Will you stop? If so, go to **59**. Or will you try to get away (go to **38**)?

4

'Look, there's a man in the Tower of London, and he is here with his gang to steal the crown jewels,' you tell the guard.

'Don't be daft! This place has had hundreds of bad men in it and they're all gone. No one would be fool enough to try and steal the crown jewels. I think you're lying to me. Now what exactly are you doing?' the guard shouts.

'I can't tell you that,' you reply.

'You'll tell me now,' he says. As his finger begins to squeeze the trigger of his rifle you see strange shapes pass before your eyes and you feel yourself falling, falling, falling.

You find yourself on the floor of the time chamber and see Colonel Strong's face peering through the glass. Your mission is over. Strong promised that you would not come to any harm and he has kept his promise. The colonel opens the door and helps you to your feet.

'It seems I've failed. I couldn't tell the guard anything. It would have made things very complicated. But we could try it all again, couldn't we?' you ask the colonel.

If you would like to try the mission once again, go back to **1**.

5

'Yes, I do know Colonel Strong,' you say, quickly realising that you've made a terrible mistake. 'Wasn't he a famous soldier in the Zulu war? I don't exactly know him, but I've seen him.'

'Don't lie to me. You know Colonel Strong runs F.E.A.R. and you work for him,' spits Triton, convinced that you are a F.E.A.R. agent.

'I'm not, I'm not,' you stumble.

You quickly need to think of something to convince him. Have you got a pocket watch? If you have, you could give it to Triton and tell him that you stole it. That's bound to make him think that you are a child thief. If you have got the watch, go to **86**. If you have not got the watch, you must go to **80**.

6

Triton pushes past you as you step out of the doorway. He runs straight over to the boxes of jewels and crowns, opening each one in turn and stuffing precious gems, pearls and gold into his pockets. He then opens the box containing the crown and knocks his hat off onto the floor. He jams the crown onto his bald head.

Carefully and quietly you take the key out of the lock, close the door and lock it from the outside. You then throw the key to the other side of the room.

'Now, exactly what are you going to do?' you say calmly to Triton.

'Let me out! Get that key and let me out!' he screams.

'I'll do it if you give me your time chip,' you tell him, snatching the crown from his head.

'I don't suppose I have much choice,' he says, stuffing his hand in his pocket and allowing jewels and gold to spill out onto the floor.

Triton holds the time chip in his hand and you walk over and pick up the key, pretending that you are about to give it to him. As you reach the door, instead of passing him the key you snatch the time chip out of his hand.

'Bye bye, Triton. See you in another place, in another time,' you smile.

You drop the time chip onto the floor and stamp on it. As you look up you see Triton's body flickering before he finally disappears. Now go to **100**.

7

You hope Frankie will do something, even though you haven't had a chance to talk to her yet. You join the rest of Triton's gang in the house. They have already begun to have a party to celebrate. Many of the gang are wearing the jewellery they stole and from somewhere Triton has found a red cloak and is walking around as if he were the king of England.

Suddenly you hear glass shatter and the door being kicked in. In seconds the house is full of policemen and soldiers. There are gunshots, shouts and people running in every direction. You see Triton running towards the back door and then, in front of you, you see a soldier pointing his gun at you. Will you give yourself up (go to **71**)? Or will you run after Triton. If so, you should go to **89**.

8

You are one of about ten children that will be joining Triton and his henchmen on the robbery of the Tower of London. Triton wants to attack just after dark tonight.

In the afternoon you find yourself sitting near Triton, who is looking at a map of the Tower of London. You have a chance to find

out a little more about why he wants to steal the crown jewels. Will you ask Triton why he wants to steal them? If so, go to **96**. Or will you decide not to ask Triton but to ask one of his henchmen? If so, go to **70**.

9

'He's got my granddad's medal,' you lie to the soldier, hoping that this will convince him.

'Your granddad's medal? Well you'd better get it. You can't have him walking off with that,' says the soldier.

You thank the soldier and just as you turn to go inside the house you see Triton standing in the doorway. He is handcuffed and is being dragged along by two policemen.

'Let the child search him first,' shouts the soldier to the policemen.

They stop and you walk up to Triton, flicking on your chip locator in your pocket. You hide it in your hand and run it over Triton's body. You find the time chip in his trouser pocket. You grab it and hold it in your hand.

'I worked for F.E.A.R. all along and now all your plans are ruined,' you whisper in Triton's ear.

Triton is about to say something, but grits his teeth instead and is dragged down the stairs, across the pavement and thrown into the back of a police carriage. You walk up to the carriage and peer inside at him.

'Bye bye, Triton, see you in another time and in another place. Isn't it about time you gave all this up?'

With that you drop the time chip to the floor and grind it under your heel. Still staring at Triton you see his body flicker. He lets out a moan and then disappears. You smile and walk around the corner, out of sight. Now turn to **100**.

10

You open the box, pick up the crown and begin to walk back towards the bars. Triton has a broad smile across his face. In a moment he will have exactly what he wants. Will you pass it through the bars to him? If so, go to **30**. Or will you put the crown back in the box and disobey Triton? If so, go to **33**.

11

'I wanted to drop some money off at my mother's house. She hasn't got much money you know,' you lie.

'Well, it is too foggy and far too dangerous out here at night. Get back to the house and get some sleep. I won't mention this to anyone else,' says the man.

Now go to **99**.

12

You make a grand entrance into Victorian London, falling straight onto an enormous pile of potatoes at the back of a market stall.

'Oi, what you doing with my spuds?' shouts an angry market trader.

'Sorry, I fell over,' you reply.

'Get on with you!' the market trader shouts.

You brush yourself off as best as you can and walk towards a huge crowd of people. The market is packed with shoppers, traders and stall owners. There are noises and movement everywhere. How on Earth are you going to find Frankie in all of this? Looking at the people around you, you can now see that the colonel was right. Your ragged and dirty clothes fit in perfectly.

Will you wander around and try to find Frankie? If so, go to **24**. Or will you try to find someone to ask whether they know Frankie? If so, go to **79**.

13

Catching the rest of his gang unawares, you turn around and sprint through them and out of the door. You run down the stairs, hoping that someone will come to help you. Outside everything is in darkness, apart from a fire in the distance, where you can see figures running backwards and forwards with buckets of water. You need to attract their attention. Do you have the whistle? If you do have the whistle,

turn to **28**. If you do not have the whistle, turn
to **53**.

14

'Come back, come back! You'll never make it!'
shouts one of the boys.

You ignore him and continue swimming, but
the river is running very strongly and you can
feel yourself being swept into the middle of the
river. You can barely keep afloat and all of
your strength is disappearing. As your head
dips under the water you suddenly see strange
shapes pass before your eyes and you feel
yourself falling, falling, falling.

You find yourself on the floor of the time
chamber and see Colonel Strong's face peering
through the glass. Your mission is over. Strong
promised that you would not come to any
harm and he has kept his promise. The colonel
opens the door and helps you to your feet.

'It seems I've failed,' you say.

'Yes, but that was a brave thing to do. The river is a very dangerous place.'

'But we could try it all again, couldn't we?' you ask the colonel.

If you would like to try the mission once again, go back to **1**.

15

You walk up to Triton and tap him on the shoulder.

'Excuse me, mister. I've come to join your gang,' you say.

Triton turns around with a broad grin on his face. He looks you up and down and seems to think for a moment.

'It's a F.E.A.R. agent, boys. Grab him!' he shouts.

You've got to think fast. Will you run? If so, go to **62**. Or will you stand your ground and tell him that you don't know what he's talking about (turn to **32**)?

16

You decide to do nothing about the boy and in a moment he disappears into the crowd and is lost from view. You continue to walk through the market. Suddenly, you feel a hand on your shoulder.

'Gotcha!' announces a voice.

You spin around and see a policeman.

'I haven't done anything!' you yell.

'I just saw your mate nick something from that gent,' the policeman says, looking straight into your eyes.

'I don't know what you're talking about,' you protest.

'You don't expect me to believe that. All you kids around here are thieves. You're coming with me to the station,' says the policeman.

Will you try to get away from the policeman? If so, go to **2**. Or will you let the policeman lead you away? If so, go to **31**.

17

You leave the others and head off to try to find Triton. You know he must be somewhere near the old Jewel Tower, but you are not sure where it is and the Tower of London is a very big place.

You see someone walking along, just a few metres in front of you. He is one of the guards and he hasn't spotted the fire yet. Will you hide until he passes? If so, go to **64**. Or will you run up to him and tell him what is going on? If so, turn to **66**.

18

'Thank you for dropping your gun. But I'm still not going to let you have this key,' you say, teasing Triton.

'Give me the key! You promised that you would give me the key!' he screams back at you.

'I'll open the door if your gang backs off,' you shout back.

'Back! Out!' he barks to his men.

As the last of Triton's henchmen leaves the Jewel Room you unlock the barred, iron door. Will you stay where you are and let him join you? If so, go to **6**. Or will you walk out and let him go in on his own? If so, go to **41**.

19

The old tower seems deserted as Triton leads his band of thieves up the stairs towards the Jewel Room. Triton approaches the door and two of his henchmen charge ahead to force the lock. They break the lock off with iron bars and push the door open.

Triton steps into the room, followed by his men. You follow at the rear, thinking and waiting for a chance to stop him. Part of the room is blocked off with iron bars and a heavy, iron door. Everyone is staring through the bars at the boxes of jewels and crowns.

'I need someone to squeeze through those bars and pass the jewels through,' says Triton.

He turns and faces you.

'You're ideal – just the right size,' he says to you.

Will you obey Triton and squeeze through the bars? If so, you should go to **68**. Or will you refuse, as you feel you cannot let him steal the crown jewels? If so, you should go to **27**.

20

'I'm very frightened and I just want to go home,' you tell the guard.

'Now, now, don't get yourself all upset. Make sure you stay here. I'll go and get the captain,' the guard says to you.

The guard turns around and disappears into the night. No sooner has he turned a corner than Triton and the rest of them join you.

'Good work! Now let's get into that tower and grab those jewels,' says Triton.

Triton leads the gang towards the tower, opens the door and you all step inside. Now go to **19**.

21

You run towards the house. There are soldiers and policemen everywhere. Some have already captured members of Triton's gang and have handcuffed them and are dragging them off to waiting police carriages. As you reach the door you hear someone yell at you.

'Stop exactly where you are or I will shoot!'

You spin around and see a soldier pointing his rifle at you. Will you ignore him? If so, go to **58**. Or will you obey him (go to **94**)?

22

Your group runs off back towards Traitors' Gate and you see several shadowy figures emerging from the darkness. At the head of the group is Triton, who has placed the crown of England on his head. All of the others have other crowns or boxes of jewels. He seems to have got away with it. There may be a chance later to stop him. Now go to **43**.

23

You move over so that you are sitting at the edge of the boat and with all your weight and strength you begin rocking the boat. There are shouts and some of the people are panicking, but not Triton.

'Everybody keep still!' he shouts.

No sooner has he said this than you fall into the water. There is a strong current and the water is filthy. Will you call for help? If so, go to **37**. Or will you try to swim for the bank (go to **14**)?

24

At first you are swept along by the crowds, but then learn to push and shove to move in the direction you want to go. Among the crowd are many poor people, but there are also richer people around and these seem to be attracting the attention of children. They are all dressed in rags and seem to be working as a group. One of them brushes up against a lady carrying a basket of shopping and then moves away from her, bumping into another child. You think they may have stolen something from the lady. As you walk along you see a small boy in front of you, walking very close to a man dressed in a long overcoat.

He has a bowler hat on his head and looks very rich. Suddenly you see the boy dip his hand into the man's pocket and pull something out. In a split second the boy has turned away and is pushing himself through the crowd, away from the man.

Will you ignore this? If so, go to **16**. Or will you try to stop the boy, who has obviously stolen something from the man? If so, go to **35**.

25

As Triton's eyes continue to swirl around, you cannot stop yourself from falling completely under his control.

'Give … me … the … chip … locator,' you hear, as if someone is talking to you from far away.

You cannot resist reaching into your pocket and taking out the chip locator. You hold it out for Triton. Just as his hand reaches out to grab it you see strange shapes pass before your eyes and you feel yourself falling, falling, falling.

You find yourself on the floor of the time chamber and see Colonel Strong's face peering through the glass. Your mission is over. Strong promised that you would not come to any harm and he has kept his promise. The colonel opens the door and helps you to your feet.

'It seems I've failed,' you say, stumbling over your words, still suffering from the effects of Triton's hypnotic eyes.

'Yes, Triton had hypnotised you and we couldn't allow him to get the chip locator. You'll recover really quickly,' the colonel tells you.

'Give me a few minutes, and then we could try it all again, couldn't we?' you ask.

If you would like to try the mission once again, go back to **1**.

26

You decide to ask the flower lady. She doesn't seem particularly busy and most of her flowers have already been sold. She looks very cold.

'Yes, dearie?' she says as you walk up to her.

'I wondered if you knew Frankie?' you ask.

'Yes, she sells flowers too. She's just around the corner from here. Is she your sister or something?' the flower lady asks you and points to the right.

'Sort of. Thanks,' you reply.

You rejoin the crowd and manage to push your way along until you see a brown-haired, green-eyed girl with a shawl wrapped around her shoulders, selling a dozen red roses to a man in a top hat. This must be Frankie. Now turn to **60**.

27

'I won't do it,' you say to Triton.

'Oh, but you will,' Triton replies. 'I brought all of you along to do exactly as I say. Now look into my eyes.'

He has a strange expression on his face and his eyes seem to be fixed to yours. Will you stare back into his eyes? If so, go to **34**. Or will you look away (go to **39**)?

28

Triton's men are spilling out of the door and running towards you. Triton appears at the doorway. He looks very angry and he's shaking his fist at you. You place the whistle to your lips and blow several long, piercing blasts.

You glance over to see the men dealing with the fire and see that they have heard the noise and are running towards you. In minutes Triton's gang is surrounded and more soldiers are appearing. Two of them grab Triton by his arms and drag him off.

You need to get hold of Triton's time chip, so you chase after them.

'He's got something of mine and I want it back,' you say.

'Well, I suppose you did save the crown jewels,' replies one of the soldiers. 'Go ahead and search him, but make it quick.'

You turn on your chip locator and keep it hidden in your hand. You run it over Triton's  body. He is cursing and swearing at you, but you ignore him and continue. You find the chip in the inside pocket of his overcoat and snatch it.

It would be difficult to explain Triton's disappearance now if you were to smash the time chip, so you must wait until Triton is locked away in one of the cells. You follow the two men, who are half dragging Triton to the prison cell.

'Can I just have a few words with him before I go?' you ask.

'Yes, of course, but don't take too long about it,' the soldier replies. He locks the door and moves off.

'Well, Triton it seems you've failed to steal the crown jewels,' you say through the bars, dropping his time chip onto the ground.

'I suppose there's nothing else to say but goodbye,' he growls, staring straight into your face.

With that you grind the time chip into the stone floor under your foot. Triton's body flickers, he lets out one last moan and then disappears. Now turn to **100**.

29

'Is everything ready?' shouts the colonel.

All of the agents and scientists in the back of the truck give their thumbs up and you hear the time machine powering up, ready to send you back to 1881.

'Just one last thing, Colonel – what does Frankie look like?' you ask.

'She's about 13, quite tall with brown hair and green eyes. This is only her second mission, so she'll be relying on you,' Colonel Strong tells you.

You shake hands with the colonel, then step inside the chamber and take a deep breath. Suddenly the chamber feels as if it is spinning around and around. The control room is swirling and fading, and different shapes are appearing in front of your eyes. You hear a strange, whooshing sound, like a strong wind. You keep spinning and then you feel yourself falling. Now turn to **12**.

30

You carry the crown to the bars and pass it through into Triton's eager hands. He knocks his top hat off and onto the ground and jams the crown onto his bald head.

'All bow down before King Triton!' he shouts.

Many of his gang obey him, although they look very confused.

'Now, F.E.A.R. agent – yes, I know you are one – how sweet of you, how kind to help me take the crown. And what is more, you'll be trapped in there. The guards will find you and you'll get the

blame for the missing crown,' he laughs. 'Boris, bend those bars so he can't get out!'

One of Triton's muscle men walks forwards

and bends the bars until they are almost
joined.

'Goodbye, F.E.A.R. agent,' he shouts back
to you.

And with that the whole gang leaves the
room and you are left alone. Suddenly you see
strange shapes pass before your eyes and you
feel yourself falling, falling, falling.

You find yourself on the floor of the time
chamber and see Colonel Strong's face peering
through the glass. Your mission is over. Strong
promised that you would not come to any
harm and he has kept his promise. The colonel
opens the door and helps you to your feet.

'It seems I've failed. Triton has the crown
and with it he can change history. I must go
back and start again!' you shout to the colonel.

To restart the mission, go back to **1**.

31

You might have a chance, because the
policemen in those days were not very well

paid. You don't have any money, but if you have the pocket watch you could offer to give it to him if he lets you go. If you do have the pocket watch with you, go to **83**. If you do not have the pocket watch, then you should go to **67**.

32

'What's one of those?' you say, trying to keep a puzzled look on your face.

'So you don't know what a F.E.A.R. agent is? But I bet you know someone called Colonel Strong, don't you?' Triton asks.

Will you tell him that you know Colonel Strong? If so, go to **5**. Or will you lie and tell him that you've never heard of Colonel Strong? If so, go to **49**.

33

'If you want it, come and get it!' you scream, diving behind the boxes of jewels.

As you hit the ground you see a key lying on

the floor. You snatch it up, wondering whether or not it is a key to the iron door, which is between you and Triton's gang. You hear a shot whistle above your head as Triton desperately fires at you.

'I've got the key to the door. If you drop your gun I'll give you the key and you can take everything,' you shout, bravely standing up and confronting Triton.

'All right, I'll do it,' he replies grumpily and his gun clatters to the floor.

Will you give him the key? If so, go to **74**. Or will you refuse to give him the key? If so, go to **18**.

34

You stare into Triton's eyes. They appear to be swirling around and you are beginning to feel very odd, almost as if you are not yourself. He must be trying to control you. Will you continue to stare into his eyes? If so, you should go to **25**. Or will you try to look away (go to **39**)?

35

If you have your walking stick you could try to trip up the boy. Otherwise it will be very difficult to catch him. If you have a walking stick, turn to **36**. If you do not have a walking stick, turn to **65**.

36

With your walking stick at the ready, you plunge into the crowd after the boy. He is just ahead of you and you hook his leg with the stick and he falls onto the cobbled street. You pounce on him and pin him down.

'Give it back. Give it to me now!' you demand.

The little boy can only be six or seven years old. He is dirty and scared, but he hands over a leather wallet, which he has taken from the man's pocket. As you hold the wallet the little boy squirms away from you and runs off. You stand up to see the man towering over you. He is smiling at you as you hand over the wallet.

'I'm very grateful to you,' the gentleman says.

'It was nothing,' you reply.

The man extends his hand to shake yours.

'My name is Nicholas Fantom. I'm a newspaper reporter and I know my way around this city. Is there anything I can do to help you?' he asks.

'I'm trying to find a group of child thieves. They are supposed to be based somewhere near here,' you tell the man.

'I wouldn't get involved with that lot. But I can give you an address. Try 47 Old Compton Street. Make sure you keep your wits about you. There's a very odd man that leads the gang. Someone told me his skin was green, if you believe that!' the man warns you.

'Thanks,' you reply.

And with that the man walks away and disappears into the crowd.

There's no point in wasting time trying to find Frankie. Hopefully you can get a message to her later, but you have an important lead and you decide to make for the house straight away.

Old Compton Street is fairly easy to find and sure enough there are children going in and out of number 47. This could be where Triton is hiding.

If you want to go in and try to join the gang, go to **72**. If you would prefer to wait outside and see if you can spot Triton, go to **57**.

37

'Help, help! Get me out!' you scream.

Triton himself holds out an oar for you to grab hold of.

'I'll pull you back aboard,' he shouts.

Perhaps he isn't all that bad? Triton drags you back into the boat. The small boat is still rocking. Will you try to sink it once more, even though you know it is very dangerous? If you want to try it again, go to **95**. If you would prefer to stay in the boat and tell Triton that you slipped out, go to **61**.

38

The fog is very thick and you are still being followed, as you can hear voices some distance behind you. You have no hope of finding Frankie. You continue walking for a few more minutes and then you see a police station up ahead. Perhaps if you told the police what you have just learned then Triton could be stopped. Do you want to go into the police station? If so, go to **84**. Or will you give up and turn back, hoping that you can stop Triton later? If so, go to **82**.

39

'I told you to look into my eyes!' Triton shouts, in a frustrated way.

You turn your head away and refuse to look at him.

'I'll give you one last chance. Either you go through those bars or you'll never get out of this tower alive,' he screams.

Will you obey him now and go through the bars? If so, go to **68**. Or will you try to run off? If so, go to **13**.

40

'Don't shoot!' you say. 'Someone is trying to steal the crown jewels.'

You can barely get the sentence out before you hear a gunshot and see strange shapes pass before your eyes and you feel yourself falling, falling, falling.

You find yourself on the floor of the time chamber and see Colonel Strong's face peering through the glass. Your mission is over. Strong promised that you would not come to any harm and he has kept his promise. The colonel opens the door and helps you to your feet.

'It seems I've failed. I can't blame the guard. He didn't know who I was or what I was doing there. But we could try it all again, couldn't we?' you suggest to the colonel.

If you would like to try the mission once again, go back to **1**.

41

'Just let me get out first,' you say to Triton.

He obeys you and backs off. You unlock the door and push it open, then step into the main room. Now turn to **47**.

42

The four of you run outside just in time to see Triton being bundled into a prison carriage.

'Stop! I need to search that man,' you say.

The soldiers and policemen stop and stare at you, unsure of what to do.

'Do as he tells you. Bring him over here,' barks one of the scientists.

They drag Triton towards you. He has a miserable expression on his face and realises that he has been beaten. You switch on your

chip locator and run it over him, finding his chip in his trouser pocket.

'Thanks and goodbye,' you say, dropping the chip to the pavement and stamping on it.

To everyone's amazement, Triton's body flickers and then disappears.

'Blimey! He must have been a ghost!' exclaims one of the policemen.

'Well, sort of,' you reply, walking away.

The four of you disappear around a corner, out of sight of the policemen and soldiers. Now turn to **100**.

43

Triton is very excited and delighted that he has succeeded in getting the crown of England.

'Everyone from now on will call me King Triton,' he announces in a loud voice.

His henchmen look confused, but they too are very happy with all of the jewels and gold that they have stolen. The boats take the same route back along the river to the jetty, where the carriages are waiting. Everyone is in high spirits and Triton is overjoyed that his plan has worked. Eventually you arrive back at Old Compton Street and everyone piles out of the carriages and into the house.

Across the other side of the road you recognise Frankie. She has been watching the house for hours. Will you try to slip across the road and tell her what has happened? If so, go to **54**. Or will you decide that it is too risky at the moment (go to 7)?

44

'It's a scientific thing. He can do terrible damage with it. He could even take over the world,' you start to explain to the soldier.

'Rubbish! What are you talking about? Nothing in the world could do that!' he replies. 'You stay here until someone can tell me who you are, otherwise you will join the rest of them in the prison cells.'

To your horror you see Triton appear in the

doorway. He is bareheaded and looks very miserable. It is then that you realise he, too, has been captured and is in handcuffs. But there is nothing that you can do to get the time chip.

'You'd better join the others until I'm able to find out exactly who you are,' says the soldier.

You are bundled into the back of a carriage with bars at the door, and as you sit alone and in silence you realise that you came very close to beating Triton.

Suddenly you see strange shapes pass before your eyes and you feel yourself falling, falling, falling.

You find yourself on the floor of the time chamber and see Colonel Strong's face peering through the glass. Your mission is over. Strong promised you that you would not come to any harm and he has kept his promise. The colonel opens the door and helps you to your feet.

'It seems I've failed,' you say.

'Don't worry, I'll send someone back to 1881

and they can search Triton in prison and destroy his time chip,' replies the colonel.

But if you would like to try again, go back to **1**.

45

You slip into one of the buildings and see several doors in front of you. Although you have no idea what is behind any of these doors, you can see that each of them has a little latch. You close the latch and fix the padlocks as you were told and then run back outside to meet up with the other children.

'Right – now we've got to set fire to that other building,' says one of the boys, who is obviously a leader.

'Why?' you ask.

'So we can slip out in the confusion and the boss won't be bothered,' he replies.

Will you help them start the fire? If so, go to **78**. Or will you slip away from them and try to join up with Triton? If so, go to **77**.

46

Triton leads his henchmen and child thieves onto the pavement. Waiting alongside is a fleet of horse-drawn carriages. You climb onboard the second one so that you can keep an eye on Triton, who is in the front carriage.

In the dimming light the carriages weave their way through the streets until they reach the bank of the River Thames. You are ordered to get out of the carriages and follow Triton onto a jetty, where there are three boats waiting for you.

You decide to get into the boat that Triton has chosen. One of the boys pushes the boat off from the jetty and two of Triton's men start rowing away from the bank.

There could be a chance here to stop Triton before he even starts his robbery. Do you want to try to rock the boat and sink it? If so, go to **23**. Or do you think that this is a bad idea and that you may have a better chance later? If so, go to **90**.

47

Without the policeman noticing, you bring your stick around and push it between his ankles. He falls over onto the cobbles and his hat tumbles into the crowd, where it is trodden on three or four times before he can reach it. He is shouting and yelling, but he has let go of you. You run off into the crowd knowing that he has very little hope of finding you.

Having had a close brush with the law, you need to find Frankie quickly and get out of the area. You notice a lady flower seller just up ahead and decide to ask her whether she knows Frankie. Now go to **26**.

48

You walk up to the policeman. He is a large, red-faced man with an enormous moustache. He looks friendly enough, but his eyes are constantly on the move, looking for trouble.

'Excuse me, you wouldn't happen to know someone called Frankie? She works on this

market somewhere and she is a
friend of mine,' you ask.

'There are hundreds
working here. Never heard
of her. And what are you
doing here anyway?
Up to no good I bet,' the
policeman says.

'No, I'm just looking for
my friend Frankie,' you reply.

'Well I don't know her, and you stay out of
trouble,' the policeman says, walking off.

Well, the policeman was not much use, so
will you continue to wander around, hoping
that you might find Frankie? If so, go to **24**. Or
will you go and ask a lady that is selling flowers
close by? If so, go to **26**.

49

'I don't know what a F.E.A.R. agent is and I've
never heard of Colonel Strong. Is he in the
army?' you lie.

'Well, kind of,' says Triton. 'If you don't know what I'm talking about then I suppose you're OK. Go and grab yourself something to eat and come to the meeting in the cellar at nine o'clock. That's only half an hour from now, so don't be late.'

With that Triton turns and walks up the steps into the house. You follow him, keeping some distance in case he changes his mind. There are several boys eating food in the kitchen and you manage to grab some bread and milk. In next to no time everyone is leaving to head for the cellar and you follow, down the dark steps under the stairs into a huge room full of child thieves. Now turn to **76**.

50

Although it is difficult to see anything in the half-light, you continue to wait in case the man turns around. After a few minutes you are rewarded and he does turn around. You cannot mistake that green skin. It is Triton, exactly as you saw him in the photograph Colonel Strong showed you. There is no real option. You have to get in with the gang to find out what is going on.

You stand up and calmly walk across the road towards Triton, determined to persuade him that all you want to do is to become one of his many thieves. Now turn to **15**.

51

You stand in the darkness for a few moments, wondering what to do. Then, way off to the other side of the Tower of London, you see figures moving around near a fire, which was started by Triton's gang. They are desperately trying to put out the fire with buckets of water. Triton appears in the doorway of the old Jewel Tower and he has the crown of England on his head. He spots you and barks an order to two of his henchmen. 'Get him! And throw him into the River Thames!'

The two men run over and drag you towards Traitors' Gate. Just as they pitch you into the water from the walls of the Tower you see strange shapes pass before your eyes and you feel yourself falling, falling, falling.

You find yourself on the floor of the time chamber and see Colonel Strong's face peering through the glass. Your mission is over. Strong promised you that you would not come to any harm and he has kept his promise. The colonel opens the door and helps you to your feet.

'It seems I've failed. Triton has the crown of England and with it he can change history. I must go back and start the mission all over again!' you plead with the colonel.

To start the mission again, go back to **1**.

52

You take a long, hard look at the three options and finally decide to take the walking stick.

'I think I'll take the walking stick,' you say.

'Probably a good choice. It could be useful to defend yourself in a tight spot,' agrees the colonel.

'And for reaching things,' you reply.

'Yes, that too. Now we'd better get you ready to go,' says the colonel.

Turn to **29**.

53

You run towards the flickering flames and the group of men carrying the buckets of water. You have barely got halfway when one of Triton's men grabs you around the legs and you fall to the ground. The henchman turns you over and you look up to see Triton staring down at you.

'Well I always suspected you were a F.E.A.R. agent, but you won't stop me,' he sneers at you. 'Now I'm going to take that chip locator and see if it might be of some use to me in the future.'

As his hand reaches down to search you for the chip locator, you see strange shapes pass before your eyes and you feel yourself falling, falling, falling.

You find yourself on the floor of the time chamber and see Colonel Strong's face peering through the glass. Your mission is over. Strong promised you that you would not come to any harm and he has kept his promise. The colonel opens the door and helps you to your feet.

'It seems I've failed. I couldn't let Triton control me with his hypnotic eyes. But we could try it all again, couldn't we?' you ask Colonel Strong.

If you would like to try the mission once again, go back to **1**.

54

No one takes any notice of you as you run across the road to where Frankie is standing.

'Triton's got it! He's got the crown and he's stolen all the jewels too!' you explain to Frankie.

'I know. I've been tracking you all the time and you've done extremely well. Triton has got a nasty little surprise coming to him,' Frankie replies and with that she raises a whistle to her lips.

Frankie blasts three times on the whistle and out of the shadows run dozens of soldiers and policemen. They crash through the front door of the house and begin rounding up Triton's gang.

Your mission is not over. You must try to get Triton's time chip. Now turn to **21**.

55

'I've never heard of Colonel Strong. Is he a war hero or something?' you lie.

'No, he's no hero,' replies Triton, 'and if you haven't heard of him forget it. Come down to the cellar for the meeting. I'm about to make you very rich.'

You pass Triton, leaving him to shake hands with the rest of the boys who were in the line behind you, and you walk down the dark steps under the stairs into a huge room full of child thieves. Now turn to **76**.

56

The policeman doesn't even search you when you get to the police station. He just gives you a battered cup and a plate, then throws you into a large cell. Inside the cell are dozens of other children, as well as men and women, who have all been arrested for various crimes.

'You'll get your meal in three hours,' the policeman says. 'Find yourself a bed and keep quiet.'

The cell is filthy and full of rats. There is only a bucket in the corner to use as a toilet. You sit down beside one of the barred windows, wondering what to do next. A small boy comes and sits next to you.

'Are you one of us? One of the band of child thieves?' he asks.

'No, but I would like to be,' you reply. 'Where can I go when I get out of here in the morning?'

'I shouldn't really be telling you this, but it is 47 Old Compton Street,' he tells you.

This means that you don't have to search for Frankie because you have the lead you wanted. Hopefully you can get a message to Frankie later, when you've found out more about Triton's gang.

You and the boy chat for a short while, but he doesn't really know anything about Triton – not that you can ask him that directly. Your evening meal is stale bread, a thin, watery gruel soup and a cup of water. You settle down to sleep just as it is getting dark and hope that rats don't run across you in the night.

The policeman throws you out of the cell early the next morning, with a warning never to come to Covent Garden again.

You hope the boy was telling you the truth, as it is your only lead, and you head for the address he gave you. Old Compton Street is fairly easy to find and sure enough there are children going in and out of number 47. This could be where Triton is hiding.

If you want to go in and try to join the gang, go to **72**. If you would prefer to wait outside and see if you can spot Triton, go to **57**.

57

You decide to wait outside and all you see for several hours is children going in and out of the house. You manage to find a good hiding place behind some bushes. You are beginning to feel very tired and hungry, but you can't miss the chance of spotting Triton should he turn up.

Just before dark a carriage pulls up outside the house. The driver jumps off and walks around the carriage to open the door. A large, bulky figure in an overcoat and hat gets out of the carriage. You cannot see his face.

It might be Triton! Will you stay where you are? If so, go to **50**. Or will you creep across the road to try to get a better look? If so, go to **81**.

58

'No time for that, sorry,' you shout back at the soldier and push your way towards the door.

You hear a gunshot and suddenly you see strange shapes pass before your eyes and you feel yourself falling, falling, falling.

You find yourself on the floor of the time chamber and see Colonel Strong's face peering through the glass. Your mission is over. Strong promised you that you would not come to any harm and he has kept his promise. The colonel opens the door and helps you to your feet.

'It seems I've failed. I can't blame the soldier. I got so close, but he didn't know who I was or what I was doing there. But we could try it all again, couldn't we?' you ask the colonel.

If you would like to try the mission once again, go back to **1**.

59

You decide to obey the voice in the fog and wait for the guard to catch up with you.

'What are you doing outside? Didn't you hear what the boss said?' he says to you.

Will you tell him the truth? If so, go to **87**. Or will you lie to him (go to **11**)?

60

You wait for Frankie to finish serving the man and then walk up to her. She seems to recognise you before you even open your mouth.

'Hello – you made it. Colonel Strong sent you, didn't he?' Frankie says to you. 'We have to be very careful; there are members of the gang everywhere.'

'Have you found out any more?' you ask.

'All I know is that Triton is planning something big and he has been recruiting these boys to find the very best thieves in London. I've got an address – maybe you can start there. It is 47 Old Compton Street,' Frankie tells you.

'OK, that's a good plan,' you say. 'How can I keep in touch with you?'

'It's difficult without mobile phones, but I'll be keeping my eye out for you. I'll keep checking 47 Old Compton Street. Try to get to me and pass on whatever you have found out,' Frankie says.

A couple of women approach Frankie's stall wanting to buy some flowers, so you slip back into the crowd and head for the address Frankie has given you.

Old Compton Street is fairly easy to find and, sure enough, there are children going in and out of number 47. This could be where Triton is hiding.

If you want to go in and try to join the gang, go to **72**. If you would prefer to wait outside and see if you can spot Triton, then go to **57**.

61

'I must have slipped over when the boat started rocking,' you tell Triton.

'You're safe now. Someone find him some dry clothes,' he shouts to his henchmen, wrapping you up in a blanket.

The new clothes are far cleaner than the ones that you had on before, so even though your attempt to sink the boat failed, at least you feel cleaner.

The boats continue towards Traitors' Gate – the frightening gates in the river that lead straight into the Tower of London. In olden times traitors were brought to the Tower this way before they faced the executioner. Now turn to **85**.

62

You turn on your heels and run as fast as you can. By now there are dozens of them after you. You tear around the corner and try to make for an alleyway just ahead, hoping that you can lose them. As they come around the corner one of their leaders is shouting. To your horror you see a group of Triton's thieves up ahead of you, blocking the road and moving towards you. You are trapped and there is nowhere to run. As the leader of the group comes at you with a big club in his hand you suddenly see strange shapes pass before your eyes and you feel yourself falling, falling, falling.

You find yourself on the floor of the time chamber and see Colonel Strong's face peering through the glass. Your mission is over. Strong promised you that you would not come to any harm and he has kept his promise. The colonel opens the door and helps you to your feet.

'It seems I've failed. There were too many of

them for me to handle. But we could try it all again, couldn't we?' you say to the colonel.

If you would like to try the mission once again, go back to **1**.

63

The policeman has a very confused look on his face. He's not sure what to make of your story or whether you are telling the truth. As you begin to struggle to think of something that he might understand, you see a very welcome sight. Frankie appears at the door. Beside her are two men dressed in army officer uniforms. But you recognise both of them as being two of Colonel Strong's scientists.

'Release that prisoner!' orders one of the scientists.

'Who are you?' asks the policeman.

'I am General Ogilvy and the child works for me,' replies the scientist.

The policeman takes the handcuffs off you.

'We must get the chip from Triton before

he is taken away,' you tell Frankie and the scientists.

'Right – let's get out there now and find him,' says Frankie.

Now turn to **42**.

64

You decide to hide and luckily the guard doesn't see you. You wait for him to pass by and then you head off, hoping to find the Jewel Tower. You cross the main square and see a light beyond an open door. This must be it! You run towards it and sure enough, just inside, you nearly bump into Triton. Now turn to **19**.

65

With no way of stopping the boy, he slips away into the crowd and disappears from view. The man has no idea that the boy has stolen something from him and in a couple of minutes he, too, disappears into the crowd. Perhaps the boy was one of Triton's child thieves? You could have had an opportunity to have talked to him and found out more about Triton. As it is, all you can do is to continue to look for Frankie. You probably need to ask someone whether they know her. Now turn to **79**.

66

You slowly walk towards the guard and it is several seconds before he notices you.

'Halt, or I fire!' he shouts.

Will you continue walking towards him? If so, go to **40**.

Or will you dodge behind a bush and hide? If so, go to **64**.

67

There is another chance to get away, but only if you've got the walking stick. You could trip him up and make a break for it. If you do have the walking stick, go to **47**. If you do not have the walking stick, you've no option but to be carted off to spend the night in the cells (go to **56**).

68

'All right, I'll do it,' you say and with that you step forward towards the iron bars that run from floor to ceiling.

The gaps between the bars look very narrow, but somehow, with great difficulty, you manage to squeeze yourself through.

'Splendid!' Triton exclaims, clapping his fat hands with joy. 'Now walk over to the big box in front of you and get me that crown.'

The box has the official seal of Queen Victoria stamped on it. You walk over and open the box, and for a moment you just stand there, looking at the wonderful crown inside. Will you take it to Triton? If so, go to **10**. Or will you tell him you won't do it (turn to **91**)?

69

You decide to stick as close as you can to Triton. He runs off across the grounds of the Tower of London, with his henchmen and several of the child thieves. He makes straight for the old Jewel Tower. Triton crouches down behind a wall and signals for the rest of you to duck down beside him.

'There's only one guard, and I want you,' Triton whispers, pointing at you, 'to go and draw him away. Tell him you've lost something.'

You don't have much option but to obey Triton, so turn to **88**.

70

You decide not to ask Triton about his master plan and instead pick on one of the henchmen, who appear to hardly ever leave Triton's side.

'So why is the boss going to steal the crown jewels?' you ask.

'Money,' he says, patting you on the head, 'lots and lots of lovely money.'

Well that didn't work. The henchman doesn't seem to know anything, so there's not much point in asking him more. In any case, everyone now seems to be getting ready to leave for the robbery, as Triton is heading for the door. Now turn to **46**.

71

You put your hands up and a policeman rushes over and handcuffs you. The policeman searches you and finds the chip locator. This is going to take a lot of explaining.

'What is this?' the policeman asks you, pressing the buttons.

'Um, don't do that – it's dangerous,' you say.

Somehow the policeman has turned on the chip locator and you can hear it faintly buzzing, telling you that Triton is still close by.

Will you try to convince the policeman that you are not one of the gang? If so, go to **92**. Or will you say that you took the chip locator from Triton and had intended to give it to the police? If so, go to **63**.

72

You decide to go straight inside the house. The door is unlocked, so you slowly walk inside. The hallway is dark and the wallpaper is peeling off the walls. There is a horrible cooking smell and there are piles of rubbish everywhere. There is a scruffy-looking man sitting at the bottom of the stairs and he stands up as he sees you.

'What do you want? Have you got something for the boss? If you want to sleep here tonight you'd better have something good,' he snarls at you.

'I haven't got anything. I just want to join your gang,' you reply.

'What are you? A pickpocket? A burglar?' he asks.

'A bit of both,' you lie.

'The boss is always interested in good thieves, but he's told me to keep a lookout for something called F.E.A.R. agents, whatever they are. You're not a F.E.A.R. agent are you?' he asks you, leaning forward and staring straight into your eyes.

Will you tell him the truth and say that you are a F.E.A.R. agent? If so, go to **73**. Or will you tell him you don't know what he's talking about (go to **97**)?

73

'Yes, I'm a F.E.A.R. agent and I've come here to deal with your boss,' you announce.

'And I'm here to deal with you,' says the man.

With that he pulls out a club and walks menacingly towards you, swinging it in the air. Before he can strike the first blow you suddenly see strange shapes pass before your eyes and you feel yourself falling, falling, falling.

You find yourself on the floor of the time chamber and see Colonel Strong's face peering through the glass. Your mission is over. Strong promised you that you would not come to any harm and he has kept his promise. The colonel opens the door and helps you to your feet.

'It seems I've failed. Perhaps I was too honest with the man. But we could try it all again, couldn't we?' you ask the colonel.

If you would like to try the mission once again, go back to **1**.

74

You pass the key through the bars and Triton immediately opens the door. Roughly he pushes you to one side and runs over to the boxes of jewels and crowns. He is laughing and clapping his fat hands with joy. He seems to have almost forgotten you are there. You slip out of the room as all of his gang are trying to cram themselves in through the door to grab their share of the crown jewels. You run down the stairs and into the darkness. Do you have a whistle? If you do have a whistle you should turn to **28**. If you do not have a whistle you should turn to **51**.

75

You look at the three objects and finally decide to pick the whistle.

'I think I'll take the whistle,' you announce.

'Not a bad choice. It would be a good way of attracting attention or calling for help,' replies the colonel.

'That's what I thought,' you reply.

'Now we'd better get you ready,' says the colonel.

Turn to **29**.

76

Triton emerges from the stairs and walks to the front of the cellar, surrounded by his strongest henchmen. There is a board covered with cloth beside him.

'Anyone that doesn't have the guts to go through with a big job and make themselves very rich can leave now,' he starts. 'I'm going to show you something and, once I have, nobody leaves this house. Is that clear?'

One or two of the boys nod their heads, but no one moves.

'Right,' says Triton and with a flourish he pulls off the cloth from the board.

Underneath is a map and you instantly recognise it as the Tower of London. What could Triton want at the Tower of London?

'We are going to steal the crown jewels and I'm going to make each and every one of you very rich. When we get away with it everyone in this room will earn £100 each,' he says.

This is a lot of money in 1881 and everyone is very impressed.

'We are going to get into the Tower of London by the river, through Traitors' Gate. One group of you will try to make as much of a nuisance of themselves as possible by locking up the guards and setting fire to things. The rest of you will come with me to the old Jewel Tower, where we'll steal the crown jewels. Are there any questions?'

'Why are we going for something so big? It is dangerous, isn't it?' asks one of the boys.

'We all like danger, especially if the rewards are as big as this. In any case, think of the chaos it will cause if we manage to steal the crown jewels. Who knows, the whole country could fall to pieces!' replies Triton.

So that's it. He steals the crown jewels and he hopes to change history by wrecking Britain, the most powerful nation at this time in the world. The crown jewels are a symbol of the power of Great Britain. Triton obviously believes that if someone stole them nobody would take Britain seriously.

The meeting breaks up and most of the gang settle down to find something to eat and to have a rest. If you want to have a rest, go to **99**. If you want to slip out of the house and try to find Frankie to tell her, go to **3**.

77

Before the children start their fire you run off into the darkness, hoping to try to find Triton. Suddenly you see someone walking along, just a few metres in front of you. It must be one of the guards, but he hasn't spotted the fire yet. Will you hide until he passes? If so, go to **64**. Or will you run up to him and tell him what is going on? If so, turn to **66**.

78

The children have brought with them some matches and small bundles of wood. They run off towards one of the wooden buildings alongside a tower. They pile up the wood and one of them steps forward, lights a match and in a moment or two there is a bright flame in the darkness. The children run off and hide and settle down to watch the fire catch hold of the building. In a very short time the whole building is on fire.

'Come on, let's get back to Traitors' Gate,' says the leader of the children.

Will you follow them? If so, go to **22**. Or will you try to find Triton again (go to **17**)?

79

You cast your eyes around the crowd, hoping to find someone to ask about Frankie. Walking towards you is a policeman. If you want to ask him, go to **48**. Just ahead of you is a lady selling flowers. She might know Frankie. If you would prefer to ask her, go to **26**.

80

'So you know Colonel Strong,' says Triton, 'and I'm positive you're a F.E.A.R. agent. Get him, men!'

Before you can move several of Triton's men have grabbed you. As one walks towards you with a club in his hand, you suddenly see strange shapes pass before your eyes and you feel yourself falling, falling, falling.

You find yourself on the floor of the time chamber and see Colonel Strong's face peering through the glass. Your mission is over. Strong promised that you would not come to any harm and he has kept his promise. The colonel opens the door and helps you to your feet.

'It seems I've failed. Triton was bound to be suspicious, but I got very close to fooling him. We could try it all again, couldn't we?' you suggest to the colonel.

If you would like to try the mission once again, go back to **1**.

81

In the half-light you creep across the road. You still cannot see the man's face, so you must get closer. You try to flatten yourself against the railings and creep up. But suddenly the figure

that has been talking to the driver spins
around. The face is unmistakable – it is Triton
and he looks exactly like the photograph
Colonel Strong showed you.

'Get him! He must be a F.E.A.R. agent!'
screams Triton.

Several men and boys appear out of the
doorway of the house and begin running
towards you. You don't have much time.
If you want to run, go to **62**. If you want
to stand your ground and persuade Triton
that you are not a F.E.A.R. agent, go to **32**.

82

You decide to head back towards the house,
but you are spotted before you can slip
in through the window. One of Triton's
henchmen walks up to you, swinging a club
in his hand.

'What are you doing outside? Didn't you
hear what the boss said?' he says to you.

Will you tell him the truth? If so, go to **87**. Or will you lie to him (go to **11**)?

83

'If I were to give you something that was worth a lot of money, would you let me go?' you ask the policeman.

'What do you take me for? You probably nicked whatever you are going to give me anyway. What have you got?' he barks.

He grabs hold of you even more tightly and searches you, finding the pocket watch. Luckily he does not find your chip locator.

'I'll take this as, er, evidence. You're coming with me and you can spend a night in the cells.'

Now go to **56**.

84

With shadowy shapes close behind you, you pause under the lamplight outside the police station. With one last look behind, you climb the three steps to the door. You push the door inwards and walk up to the desk.

'Yes, what can I do for you?' asks the policeman at the desk.

'I want to report a robbery – well, I mean someone is planning a robbery,' you start to say.

'Really? Do tell!' replies the policeman sarcastically.

'There's a green man and a gang of child thieves and they are going to steal the crown jewels from the Tower of London,' you tell the policeman.

'Are they really?' replies the policeman, now a bit more interested.

And with that he pulls a gun from underneath the desk and points it at you.

'The boss will be very interested that he has had a spy in the house,' he says as he squeezes the trigger.

Suddenly you see strange shapes pass before your eyes and you feel yourself falling, falling, falling.

You find yourself on the floor of the time chamber and see Colonel Strong's face peering through the glass. Your mission is over. Strong promised that you would not come to any harm and he has kept his promise. The colonel opens the door and helps you to your feet.

'It seems I've failed. Triton must have bribed the policeman to work for him. But we could try it all again, couldn't we?' you ask the colonel.

If you would like to try the mission once again, go back to **1**.

85

As the boats pull alongside Traitors' Gate the gates creak inwards. Triton must have someone already inside the Tower of London and they have opened the gates for him. The boats come alongside a small, wooden jetty and everyone clambers out.

'Right – half of you go and deal with the guards and the rest of you follow me,' whispers Triton.

Will you go with the children and deal with the guards? If so, go to **93**. Or do you think it is a better idea to stay with Triton? If so, go to **69**.

86

'Take this pocket watch. I nicked it off some gent in Covent Garden,' you lie to Triton.

'Umm, interesting piece. Gold, I think, and in good working order. Very well, so you're a thief and not a F.E.A.R. agent. Take the watch back, you can earn me far more money after you've heard what our plans are at the meeting. Don't be late,' says Triton.

With that Triton turns and walks away. You follow him, keeping some distance in case he changes his mind. There are several boys eating food in the kitchen and you manage to grab some bread and milk. You wait around restlessly for the meeting to begin, but in next to no time everyone is leaving to head for the cellar and you follow, down the dark steps under the stairs into a huge room full of child thieves. Now turn to **76**.

87

'The boss has got to be stopped. We can't let him steal the crown jewels,' you answer. 'I was going to go and tell the police.'

'Were you really? I can't let you do that and

you can't be trusted.' With that reply he swings a club at you.

Suddenly you see strange shapes pass before your eyes and you feel yourself falling, falling, falling.

You find yourself on the floor of the time chamber and see Colonel Strong's face peering through the glass. Your mission is over. Strong promised you that you would not come to any harm and he has kept his promise. The colonel opens the door and helps you to your feet.

'It seems I've failed. Perhaps I would have had a better chance to stop Triton once he had reached the Tower of London. But we could try it all again, couldn't we?' you suggest to the colonel.

If you would like to try the mission once again, go back to 1.

88

Unhappy about helping Triton in any way, you feel as if you don't really have a choice.

You slip off through the darkness towards the guard. He doesn't hear you until you are just a few metres from him, but then he spins around, with his rifle at the ready and a wicked bayonet stuck on the end of it.

'Halt! Who goes there?' he shouts.

'I'm lost. I've been wandering around for ages,' you cry.

'Really?' he replies.

Will you continue to lie to the guard? If so, go to **20**. Or will you tell him the truth (go to **4**)?

89

'Stop! Stop or I'll fire!' orders the soldier.

You ignore him and easily dodge his attempts to grab you. You run into the kitchen and you can see that Triton has almost reached the back wall of the garden. He tries to heave himself up on top of the wall, but soldiers appear in front of him and then others grab his legs. In a moment he is in handcuffs and the crown of England has been ripped from his head. The soldiers and policemen are rounding up Triton's gang.

In the confusion you are grabbed and handcuffed and there is nothing you can do to

stop the police from taking Triton away. He still has the time chip with him and you cannot get it.

You are bundled into the back of a carriage with bars at the door. As you sit alone and in silence you realise that you came very close to beating Triton.

Suddenly you see strange shapes pass before your eyes and you feel yourself falling, falling, falling.

You find yourself on the floor of the time chamber and see Colonel Strong's face peering through the glass. Your mission is over. Strong promised that you would not come to any harm and he has kept his promise. The colonel opens the door and helps you to your feet.

'It seems I've failed,' you say.

'Don't worry. I'll send someone back to 1881 and they can search Triton in prison and destroy his time chip,' says the colonel.

But if you would like to try again, go back to **1**.

90

The boats make their slow progress along the River Thames, until you see a pair of huge, wooden gates in the riverbank below the Tower of London. In the old days traitors against the king or the country were brought through this gate, called Traitors' Gate, on their way to the executioner's block. Now turn to **85**.

91

'You can't have it. I won't let you have it,' you shout, turning and facing Triton.

'Oh, but I will. If you don't pass it to me right now I will shoot you, and one of the other boys will squeeze through the bars and get it for me,' he says, producing a pistol from his overcoat and pointing it at you.

Will you now obey him by picking up the crown and passing it to Triton? If so, go to **30**. Or will you disobey him (go to **33**)?

92

'I'm not one of the gang. I work for the government. I'm a spy,' you exclaim.

'Oh really, a child spy. You don't expect me to fall for that, do you?' replies the policeman.

To your amazement, Frankie appears at the door. Beside her are two men dressed in army officer uniforms. But you recognise both of them as being two of Colonel Strong's scientists.

'Release that prisoner!' orders one of the scientists.

'Who are you?' asks the policeman.

'I am General Ogilvy and the child works for me,' replies the scientist.

The policeman takes the handcuffs off you.

'We must get the chip from Triton before he is taken away,' you tell Frankie and the scientists.

'Right – let's get out there and find him,' says Frankie.

Now turn to **42**.

93

You decide to go with the children, and one of the henchmen hands you six padlocks.

'Use these to lock the doors and make sure that none of the guards can get out,' he tells you.

You scamper off after the others and follow
two of them towards one of the towers, in which
some of the soldiers guarding the Tower of
London are sleeping.

'You go that way and use your padlocks to
lock them in,' says one of the children.

Now turn to **45**.

94

You stop dead in your tracks and walk back
slowly towards the soldier.

'You don't understand. I work for the
government and we can't let the gang's boss
get away. He's got something that is really
important and I have to stop him,' you
explain.

'What's so important?' the soldier asks you.

Will you tell him the truth? If so, go to **44**.
Or will you tell him he has stolen a medal
that belonged to your grandfather? If so,
go to **9**.

95

Right next to Triton you begin to rock the boat again.

'I knew I couldn't trust you! I don't know why I saved you,' Triton says, swinging the oar at you.

You duck Triton's first attempt to knock you over the side, but the second one hits you and suddenly see strange shapes pass before your eyes and you feel yourself falling, falling, falling.

You find yourself on the floor of the time chamber and see Colonel Strong's face peering through the glass. Your mission is over. Strong promised you that you would not come to any harm and he has kept his promise. The colonel opens the door and helps you to your feet.

'It seems I've failed. I can't believe Triton actually saved me the first time,' you say to the colonel.

'Yes, that river is extremely dangerous, but it was a very brave thing to try,' the colonel replies.

'But we could try it all again, couldn't we?' you ask the colonel.

If you would like to try the mission once again, go back to **1**.

96

'Excuse me boss. If you don't mind me asking, why are you really taking the crown jewels? I know they're valuable and all that,' you ask Triton.

'Not that you'll understand, but the crown jewels represent the power and the strength of this country. A quarter of this planet belongs to the British and without the crown jewels perhaps we can bring Britain down,' Triton tells you.

You nod your head as if you are agreeing with Triton. So that's it! Triton wants to bring the British Empire down and change history. He believes that by stealing the crown jewels Britain would be the laughing stock of the world and nobody would take them seriously. You cannot allow this to happen.

'Get yourself ready,' says Triton. 'We'll be leaving very soon.'

With that Triton stands up and heads for the front door, calling his henchmen around him. Now turn to **46**.

97

'I don't know what you're talking about,' you say. 'What is a F.E.A.R. agent anyway? Are they police?'

'I don't know,' he replies, 'the boss just told me to say that. I wouldn't know what a F.E.A.R. agent was if he walked up and bit me. You'd better get yourself inside.'

You do as the man instructs and then find yourself a quiet place to have a sleep. Just before nine o'clock there is a lot of movement around the house. You wake up and see the room is full of children, all very excited, and you follow them out. At the bottom of the stairs is a man in a top hat and an overcoat. He is shaking hands with each of the children as they pass. In a minute it will be your turn.

'Welcome, welcome. We're all going to be very rich, providing we keep our wits about us,' says the man in the coat.

You look up and stare him in the face. It is unmistakably green and it is Triton.

'I've not seen you around here before. Do you know a friend of mine, Colonel Strong?' Triton asks you.

Will you tell him that you do know who Colonel Strong is? If so, go to **5**. Or will you tell him that you have never heard of Colonel Strong (go to **55**)?

98

After thinking for a couple of minutes you decide to choose the pocket watch.

'I think I'll take the pocket watch. Does it do anything special?' you ask.

'No, it's too dangerous to take anything advanced back to 1881. We're taking a risk with the chip locator anyway,' replies the colonel.

'OK,' you reply, rather disappointed that it doesn't do anything neat like fire a laser beam.

'Now we'd better get you ready to leave,' says the colonel.

Now turn to **29**.

99

After eating a bowl of revolting, lukewarm, watery porridge and gulping down some water, you find a room that isn't too crowded and wrap yourself up in a blanket. You drift off to sleep.

In the morning Triton has had a cook come in and she has made porridge for everyone. This is the first decent food you've had since you have arrived in 1881 and it makes you feel much warmer and stronger. It seems as if the rest of the day will be taken up with preparing for the robbery at the Tower of London, so now turn to **8**.

100

With your mission complete, you are ready to head back to your own time and place. Sure enough, just as you are safely out of sight, you feel yourself falling, falling, falling.

You find yourself on the floor of the time chamber and see Colonel Strong's smiling face peering through the glass. You have successfully completed your mission. Strong promised that you would not come to any harm and he has kept his promise.

The colonel opens the door and helps you to your feet.

'You've done it! You've beaten him!' he exclaims.

Everyone in the truck is clapping and cheering. Your F.E.A.R. mission has been a success. You can return home, pleased with your work, until the next time of course. Who knows where Triton will strike again?

★ ★ ★

The Emerald Pirate

Triton has become the Emerald Pirate! His crew are robbing and sinking ships, collecting a vast pile of gold and treasure, but why?

YOU are sent back in time to the peaceful island of Santa Diana, known to be the Emerald Pirate's next target.

Can YOU save the islanders, battle with zombies and put a stop to the Emerald Pirate's evil plan? Solve the puzzles and find the clues in this exciting adventure into a strange pirate world.

£4.99   ISBN 1 84046 690 1

The Spy Master

Triton has become Gary Steel – a criminal mastermind!
He has kidnapped the inventor Albert Fudge and is
forcing him to build the ultimate computer to take over
the world.

Can YOU discover Steel's secret base and destroy the
computer? YOU solve the puzzles and find the clues in
this exciting adventure into the world of spies.

£4.99   ISBN 1 84046 692 8

The Space Plague

It is 600 years in the future and the inhabitants of Earth have started travelling to other galaxies.

Triton and his vile henchmen have infected the planet Rosetta, home to many humans, with a deadly plague.

YOU are sent forward in time to visit Rosetta with the only known cure. Can YOU battle with aliens to reach the distant planet on time? YOU are the settlers' only hope, but danger lurks everywhere! Solve the puzzles and find the clues in this exciting adventure into future alien worlds.

£4.99   ISBN 1 84046 694 4

Fighting Fantasy™

Fighting Fantasy™ is a brilliant series of adventure gamebooks in which YOU are the hero.

Part novel, with its exciting story, and part game, with its elaborate combat system, each book holds many adventures in store for you. Every page presents different challenges, and the choices you make will send you on different paths and into different battles.

Magic and monsters are as real as life in these sword-and-sorcery treasure hunts which will keep you spellbound for hours.

There are over 20 *Fighting Fantasy*™ titles available.

Click on www.fightingfantasygamebooks.com to find out more.

Suitable for readers aged 9 and upwards.

Fighting Fantasy™
The Warlock of Firetop Mountain

Deep in the caverns beneath Firetop Mountain lies an untold wealth of treasure, guarded by a powerful Warlock – or so the rumour goes. Several adventurers like yourself have set off for Firetop Mountain in search of the Warlock's hoard. None has ever returned. Do you dare follow them?

Your quest is to find the Warlock's treasure, hidden deep within a dungeon populated with a multitude of terrifying monsters. You will need courage, determination and a fair amount of luck if you are to survive all the traps and battles, and reach your goal – the innermost chambers of the Warlock's domain.

£4.99   ISBN 1 84046 387 2

Suitable for readers aged 9 and upwards.

Fighting Fantasy™
Eye of the Dragon

In a tavern in Fang, a mysterious stranger offers YOU
the chance to find the Golden Dragon, perhaps the
most valuable treasure in all of Allansia. But it is hidden
in a labyrinth beneath Darkwood Forest and is guarded
by the most violent creatures and deadly traps.

To begin your quest YOU must drink a life-threatening
potion, and to succeed you must find maps, clues,
artefacts, magic items, jewels and an imprisoned
dwarf.

£4.99   ISBN 1 84046 642 1

Suitable for readers aged 9 and upwards.

Football Fantasy

Football Fantasy is a stunning new series of football gamebooks in which YOU decide the outcome of the match. YOU see what a footballer would see and make the decisions he would make.

Simple to play and challenging to master, every game is different. Learn the tricks and tactics of the game and lead your team to victory.

All titles £5.99

Thames United	ISBN 1 84046 598 0
Mersey City	ISBN 1 84046 597 2
Medway United	ISBN 1 84046 599 9
Trent Albion	ISBN 1 84046 590 5
Bridgewater	ISBN 1 84046 609 X
Clyde Rovers	ISBN 1 84046 621 9
Avon United	ISBN 1 84046 622 7
Tyne Athletic	ISBN 1 84046 596 4

Suitable for readers aged 10 and upwards.